CONTENTS

KT-226-241

Words that appear in the text in bold, **like this**, are explained in the glossary.

MAP OF RENAISSANCE EUROPE IN ABOUT 1500

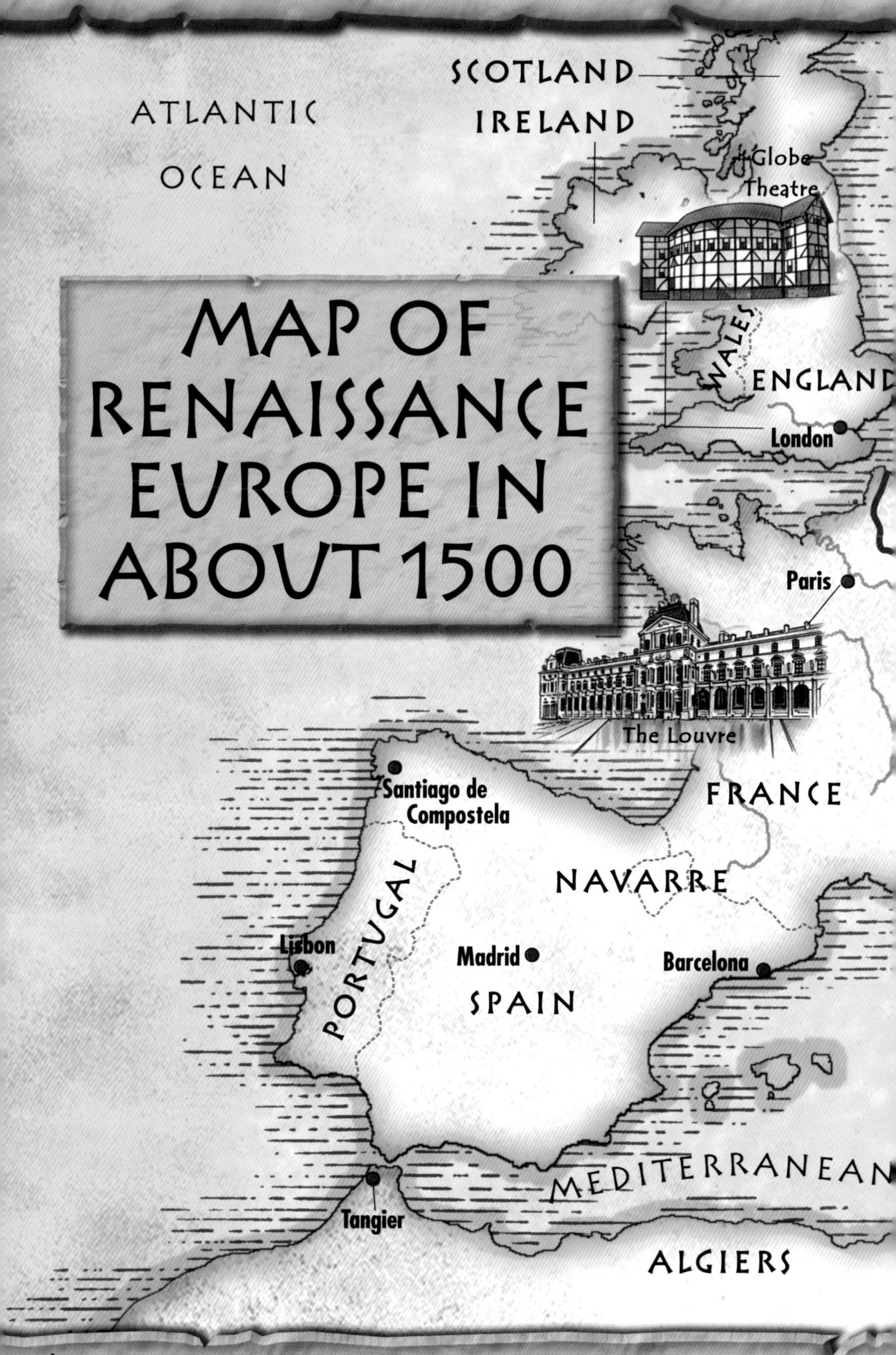

ATLANTIC

OCEAN

SCOTLAND

IRELAND

Globe
Theatre

WALES

ENGLAND

London

Paris

The Louvre

FRANCE

Santiago de
Compostela

PORTUGAL

NAVARRE

Lisbon

Madrid

Barcelona

SPAIN

Tangier

MEDITERRANEAN

ALGIERS

TIME TRAVEL GUIDES

THE RENAISSANCE

Anna Claybourne

www.raintree.co.uk/library
Visit our website to find out more information about Raintree books.

To order:
 Phone 44 (0) 1865 888112
 Send a fax to 44 (0) 1865 314091
 Visit the Raintree bookshop at www.raintree.co.uk/library to browse our catalogue and order online.

First published in Great Britain by Raintree, Halley Court, Jordan Hill, Oxford OX2 8EJ, part of Pearson Education. Raintree is a registered trademark of Pearson Education Ltd.

© Pearson Education Ltd 2008
First published in paperback 2008
The moral right of the proprietor has been asserted.

All rights reserved. No part of this publication may be reproduced, stored in a retrieval system, or transmitted in any form or by any means, electronic, mechanical, photocopying, recording, or otherwise, without either the prior written permission of the publishers or a licence permitting restricted copying in the United Kingdom issued by the Copyright Licensing Agency Ltd, 90 Tottenham Court Road, London W1T 4LP (www.cla.co.uk).

Editorial: Kathryn Walker, Sarah Shannon, Harriet Milles, and Kelly Davis
Design: Clare Nicholas and Rob Norridge
Picture Research: Amy Sparks
Illustrations: Peter Bull
Production: Duncan Gilbert
Proofreading: Catherine Clarke
Originated by Modern Age
Printed and bound in China by South China Printing Company Limited

The publishers would like to thank Professor Norman Tanner for his assistance in the preparation of this book.

ISBN 978-1-4062-099-52 (hardback)
12 11 10 09 08
10 9 8 7 6 5 4 3 2 1

ISBN 978-1-4062-100-02 (paperback)
12 11 10 09 08
10 9 8 7 6 5 4 3 2 1

British Library Cataloguing in Publication Data
Claybourne, Anna
  The Renaissance. - (Time travel guides)
  1. Renaissance - Juvenile literature
  940.2'1
A full catalogue record for this book is available from the British Library.

This levelled text is a version of *Freestyle: Time Travel Guides: The Renaissance.*

Acknowledgements
The publishers would like to thank the following for permission to reproduce photographs:
AKG p. **46**; Art Archive pp. **17** (Musée de Louvre, Paris/Dagli Orti), **19** (Dagli Orti), **23** (Art Archive), **24** (Manoir du Clos Lucé/Dagli Orti), **25** (Bibliothèque des Arts Décoratifs/Dagli Orti), **29** (National Gallery, London/Eileen Tweedy), **32** (Château de Beauregard, Val de Loire/Dagli Orti), **34** (Monte dei Paschi Bank, Siena/Dagli Orti), **42** (Bibliothèque des Arts Décoratifs/Dagli Orti), **44** (Museo Civico Cremona/Dagli Orti), **45** (Palazzo Barberini, Rome/Dagli Orti), **47** (Art Archive), **48/49** (Château de Blois/Dagli Orti) **52** (Castello di Issogne, Val d'Aosta, Italy/Dagli Orti), **53** (Biblioteca Nazionale, Marciana, Venice/Dagli Orti); Brand X Pictures pp. **10**, **12/13**; Bridgeman Art Library pp. **8** (The Stapleton Collection), **11** (Palazzo Medici-Riccardi, Florence), **14** (British Library, London), **15** (Santa Maria Novella, Florence), **18** (Palazzo Ducale, Mantua), **21** (Victoria & Albert Museum, London), **33** (Château de Versailles, France/Lauros/Giraudon), **35** (Museum Narodowe, Poznan, Poland), **36** (Castello di Issogne, Val d'Aosta, Italy/Giraudon), **38** (Christie's Images), **39** (British Museum, London), **40/41** (Galleria dell' Accademia, Venice), **51** (Giraudon), **54/55** (Galleria degli Uffizi, Florence); Corbis pp. **6/7** (Carl & Ann Purcell), **26/27** (Guenter Rossenbach/zefa), **28** (Gregor Schuster/zefa), **30** (Nik Wheeler); iStockphoto p. **22** (Ogen Perry).

Background cover photograph of Florence Cathedral reproduced with permission of Brand X Pictures. Inset photographs of map and brass globe reproduced with permission of AKG-images.

Every effort has been made to contact copyright holders of any material reproduced in this book. Any omissions will be rectified in subsequent printings if notice is given to the publishers.

NORWAY

ORTH

SEA

SWEDEN

DENMARK

TEUTONIC ORDER

MUSCOVY

TEUTONIC ORDER

HOLY ROMAN EMPIRE

POLAND

LITHUANIA

BOHEMIA

RHINE

Vienna

SAVOY

AUSTRIA

HUNGARY

MOLDAVIA

Milan

DANUBE

WALLACHIA

Venice

Genoa

Bologna

VENETIAN REPUBLIC

Florence

PAPAL STATES

Rome

KINGDOM OF NAPLES

Constantinople (Istanbul)

OTTOMAN

EMPIRE

St Peter's Basilica

N W E S

This is the Italian city of Venice. The view here has changed little since Renaissance times.

CHAPTER 1

FACTS ABOUT THE RENAISSANCE

Would you like to explore one of the most important and exciting times in European history? If the answer is yes, you should travel back to the period called the Renaissance. You will need to turn the clock back 500 years.

The Renaissance is a time of big changes in fashion, art, and music. Inventors are bursting with new ideas. European explorers are discovering the rest of the world.

Italy is the country leading the Renaissance. It is home to many of the greatest artists, scientists, and inventors of the time. Italy is definitely the best place to start your journey.

WHEN TO VISIT

The Renaissance is a period of rapid growth in learning and art. People are developing many new ideas. The Renaissance begins in Italy in the early 1400s. That's about 600 years ago. It reaches northern Europe later.

The Renaissance lasts between 200 and 300 years. It's best to visit in the late 1400s. This is when the Renaissance is at its peak in Italy.

SOME CAUSES OF THE RENAISSANCE

- Trade – More people are getting rich through trade (buying and selling goods). They have more money to spend on fashion and the arts.
- Books – The printing press is invented in the 1450s. That's about 550 years ago. Now books can be printed quickly. This means ideas can spread fast.
- Cities – New jobs draw people to the cities. Big cities become centres of learning and the arts.

This picture was made in about 1600. That's more than 400 years ago. It shows Renaissance printers at work.

- **Humanism** – Humanism means understanding the world through human ideas and experiences. Many people now think this is more important than following religious teachings.

GOOD AND BAD TIMES TO VISIT

1304–1374	Life of Italian writer Francesco Petrarch. He is known as the "father of the Renaissance".
1346–1351	The Black Death (a deadly disease) strikes northern Europe.
1420	Portuguese prince Henry the Navigator sends sailors to explore the coast of Africa.
1450s	The first printing press is invented.
1469–1492	Lorenzo de' Medici controls the Italian city of Florence. He pays for many works of art.
1492	Italian explorer Christopher Columbus sails to the Americas.
1503–1506	Italian artist Leonardo da Vinci paints his most famous painting, the *Mona Lisa*.
1509–1547	King Henry VIII is king of England. He encourages the arts and sciences in his country.
1512	Italian artist Michelangelo finishes painting the Sistine Chapel (the **pope's** chapel in the city of Rome).
1543	Polish scientist Nicolaus Copernicus explains his idea that the Earth moves around the Sun.
1564	Birth of the great English writer William Shakespeare.
1618–1648	Thirty Years War.

Key:

Stay away   Interesting times to visit   Best times to visit

WHERE TO GO

The Renaissance starts in Italy partly because of trade (business). Italy is on the Mediterranean Sea (see map on pages 4–5). Its position makes it Europe's main entry point for goods shipped in from Asia and Africa.

Because of this, Italian traders and bankers have become wealthy. They spend lots of money on beautiful houses. They also spend money on art, music, and books.

FABULOUS FLORENCE

If you're visiting in the late 1400s, Florence is the place to be. This is a beautiful city in northern Italy. At its centre is the huge cathedral. This has an amazing egg-shaped dome (curved roof).

This is the famous dome on Florence's cathedral.

DON'T FORGET THE TRIPS!

Of course, there's more to the Renaissance than just Florence. You could visit the wealthy city of Venice in Italy. You could go to the city of London in England. London is home to the great **playwright** William Shakespeare.

You could also visit the countries of Spain and Portugal. This is where many explorers set sail. They are looking for new lands.

MEET THE MEDICIS

In Renaissance Florence, the Medicis are the richest and most powerful family. In the late 1400s, Lorenzo de' Medici controls Florence. He is known as Lorenzo the Magnificent.

Lorenzo loves paintings, poetry, and science. He spends lots of money on art and science projects. This painting shows Lorenzo as a young man.

This is the Italian city of Siena, near Florence. Renaissance city-dwellers lived in surroundings that looked like this.

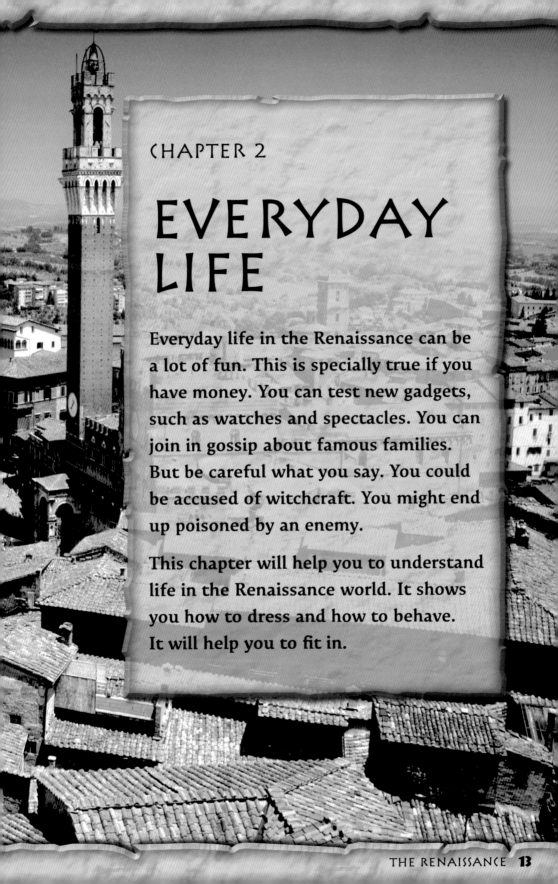

CHAPTER 2

EVERYDAY LIFE

Everyday life in the Renaissance can be a lot of fun. This is specially true if you have money. You can test new gadgets, such as watches and spectacles. You can join in gossip about famous families. But be careful what you say. You could be accused of witchcraft. You might end up poisoned by an enemy.

This chapter will help you to understand life in the Renaissance world. It shows you how to dress and how to behave. It will help you to fit in.

WHAT TO WEAR

Florence is famous for its fine fabrics and fashions. You'll have no problem finding something glamorous to wear. This guide shows you some typical clothes from the late 1400s. That's just over 500 years ago.

FASHION FOR MEN AND BOYS

A well-dressed man usually wears a **doublet**. This is a fitted waistcoat or jacket. Or he might wear a loose-fitting garment belted at the waist, called a tunic. Underneath is a loose shirt and tight-fitting leggings.

Over the top goes a cloak and a soft hat. Men have shoulder-length hair. They are clean-shaven.

This picture shows how men dressed in the Renaissance. They are wearing pointy-toed shoes. These are called poulaines. ➔

FASHION FOR WOMEN AND GIRLS

A wealthy lady wears a long, full dress. This is made of silk, wool, or velvet. She may also wear a cap or hair decoration. Dresses are often patterned or decorated with embroidery (needlework).

Women use cosmetics for colouring lips and cheeks. They use products to colour and style their hair.

This painting shows a Renaissance lady. Her dress and hairstyle are typical of the time.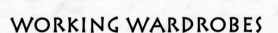

WORKING WARDROBES

Working people wear similar clothes. Men wear belted tunics with leggings. Women wear long dresses. But their clothes are much plainer. They are made of undyed cloth.

FOOD AND DRINK

Florence sets the fashion in food as well as clothes. The city has one of the first-ever cooking schools.

GRAND BANQUETS

Get yourself invited to dinner with a wealthy family. The host will try to amaze you with the latest dishes. There may be several different meats. You might even get roast swan or peacock. Expensive spices are used to flavour the sauces.

Some very modern households have forks to eat with. But many people just use a spoon or knife. Others use their hands.

EVERYDAY MEALS

In poorer households, food is simple. It's usually a stew or soup. This is made with beef and vegetables. You will have bread to dip into it. Only rich people can afford to eat pasta. It's much more expensive than bread.

Both rich and poor people drink wine. Most families grow grapes in their gardens. They use them to make their own wine every year.

TABLE MANNERS

- You can wipe your hands and mouth with a napkin. You may also use the tablecloth to do this.
- Don't pick or fiddle with your ears at the table. This is very rude.
- It's polite to share food with your neighbours. But never do this after you've taken a bite.
- After nibbling the meat off a bone, don't put the bone back on the plate. You should throw it on the floor instead.

This painting shows what a kitchen looked like about 500 years ago. The servant is busy preparing food.

HOUSES AND HOMES

There are many different types of Renaissance homes. In the country, the poorest families live in huts. In the city, they may share a single room.

Wealthier people rent a whole set of rooms. The richest have large houses or palaces.

These painted walls show the members of a wealthy Renaissance household. Even the pets are included.

Some houses and huts are made of wood. But city buildings are usually built of stone. Oil lamps provide light. Open fires heat the home. Even the smartest homes can be cold, dark, and smoky.

WINDOWS

Window glass is a new invention. Only the richest people can afford to have it. Others cover their windows with oiled cloth. Some just have a hole for a window. This can be covered up with shutters.

FURNITURE

Renaissance homes don't have much furniture. There is a table with benches or stools. There are chests for storing things. The most important piece of furniture is the bed. Often the whole family sleeps there.

Most furniture is wooden and heavy. But the rich are starting to want more beautiful furniture. They want comfortable padded chairs.

This Renaissance-style room is in the country of France. It is where the artist Leonardo da Vinci (see page 24) once lived.

RELIGION AND BELIEFS

The Catholic Church has been very powerful for a long time. This is the Christian Church led by the **pope**. The Christian Church follows the teachings of Jesus Christ. But during the Renaissance, some Christians are questioning the Church's teachings.

CHURCH WORRIES

People are worrying that some churchmen are dishonest. Some of them are failing to do their duties. But it is dangerous to question the Church. Anyone who does so can be put to death.

In 1517 a German priest speaks out against the Catholic Church. The man was Martin Luther. As a result of his attack, **Protestantism** develops. Protestantism is a new form of Christianity. It is separate from the Catholic Church. It does not have the pope as its leader.

COPERNICUS AND GALILEO

Nicolaus Copernicus (1473–1543) developed the idea that the Earth and other planets moved around the Sun. After Copernicus's death, an Italian scientist, Galileo Galilei (1564–1642) continued his work. Many in the Catholic Church were furious. The Church taught that the Earth stayed still while everything else moved around it.

HUMANISM AND SCIENCE

Humanism (see page 9) plays an big part in the Renaissance. It is a way of thinking about the world. Humanism does not accept religious explanations for everything. Instead it encourages scientists to find out how the world works.

SUPERNATURAL BELIEFS

Most people in Renaissance Europe are Christians. They also believe in many other things. In some parts of Europe, people are scared of witches. But in Italy people are happy to visit the local witch. They ask her for advice and magic spells.

This Renaissance painting shows witches casting spells. In the Renaissance, people believed anyone could secretly be a witch. →

GOVERNMENT AND POLITICS

In Renaissance times, Florence isn't just a city. It is like a small country. It is made up of Florence and the surrounding area. Most of Italy and other parts of Europe are divided in the same way. These lands are called **city-states**.

ALL-POWERFUL KINGS

Most Renaissance city-states and countries are ruled by kings and queens. Some are ruled by other powerful leaders. Their power is usually handed down through families. Sometimes leaders win their power in battles.

This building is where the Signoria in Florence was based. Renaissance Florence was ruled from here.

←

CAN YOU REACH THE TOP?

Here are a few tips on how to gain power in Florence.

- You'll need to be a member of a very rich family. If you're not already, you'll have to marry into one.
- Pay Signoria members to do what you want.
- Use your servants to spy on your enemies.
- If anyone gets in your way, you can have them poisoned.
- Spend lots of money on buildings, music, and art. The people will love you!

This painting shows a government official in the Italian city of Siena. The official carries out important work for people who rule. ➘

THE REPUBLIC OF FLORENCE

Florence is a **republic**. This means people vote for (choose) their leaders. Every two months, they choose a new Signoria. This is a group of nine people. The group's job is to run Florence.

But in Florence only rich men can vote. The real power is in the hands of great families, such as the Medicis (see page 11). These families use money and friends to control the Signoria.

NEW INVENTIONS

All over Renaissance Europe, people are inventing new gadgets. The pencil, spectacles, and the hand gun are all Renaissance inventions. People are also coming up with new ways of improving the home.

CHANGING LIFE INDOORS

A modern Renaissance home might have clear glass windows. Clear glass for windows is a Renaissance invention. Wallpaper is another new invention. People use it as a replacement for wall hangings.

LEONARDO DA VINCI

Leonardo da Vinci (1452–1519) is probably the most important Renaissance figure. He is a great artist and thinker. But he's also had brilliant ideas for inventions. This is his sketch for a helicopter-like flying machine.

RENAISSANCE INVENTIONS

These are some of the key inventions of the Renaissance:

- Spectacles: around 1280
- Clear window glass: 1400
- Hand gun: around 1430
- Printing press: 1430s
- Pencil: around 1500
- Pocket watch: around 1509
- Wallpaper: around 1510
- Thermometer: 1593
- Self-contained flushing toilet: 1594
- Telescope: 1608
- Parachute: 1617
- Submarine: 1620

This picture shows Faust Vrancic testing an early parachute. He did this almost 400 years ago.

OUTDOORS

The Renaissance is an age of exploration. There are many new inventions to help travellers. A Dutchman called Hans Lippershey invents the telescope in the 17th century. That was about 400 years ago. With a telescope you can see distant objects clearly. Another Dutchman invents the first working submarine. It is made of leather and wood.

These modern Venetians are wearing masks at the famous Venice Carnival (see page 34). Venice is a city in northern Italy. Its people have been celebrating like this for hundreds of years.

CHAPTER 3

THINGS TO SEE AND DO

Some of the most brilliant artists, musicians, and writers are at work during the Renaissance. Many of them are in Italy. This is your chance to see famous paintings, sculptures, and plays. It's also a chance to see some very beautiful buildings.

You'll find plenty of games and street entertainments here as well. There are great cafés and markets to explore. If you stayed in Florence for your whole trip, you wouldn't run out of things to do. But it's a good idea to visit other parts of Europe too. There are lots of other sights and experiences to enjoy.

ART AND ARCHITECTURE

During the Renaissance, artists move to the great cities of Europe. They go there to work for kings and other wealthy people. So do **architects**. Architects are people who design buildings.

BUILDINGS

In Florence, you can't miss the cathedral. It has an enormous dome, or curved roof. This egg-shaped dome (see picture on page 10) was designed by the architect Filippo Brunelleschi. It is typical of a new style in architecture.

This is part of a famous Renaissance building called the Louvre. This is in the country of France. Its columns are in the style of ancient Greece and Rome.

ART

Renaissance art is also going through a big change. Artists are making very realistic pictures of people and things. Leonardo da Vinci of Italy (see page 24) is one of these artists.

This is Hans Holbein's painting *The Ambassadors*. At the bottom of the painting is a strange stretched skull. You have to view the painting from exactly the right angle to see it clearly.

PATRONAGE

Patronage means paying a creative person for their work. This could be an artist or a writer. It might be a scientist or a composer of music. Patronage allows these people to do their work without worrying about money.

Many wealthy people are great **patrons**. For example, a politician (someone involved in running the country) might have an architect build a new public building. Or he may pay an artist to paint his portrait. A wealthy lady might pay for a piece of music to play at her wedding.

THE THEATRE

While you're in Renaissance Italy you could go to the theatre. Go and see a **commedia dell'arte** show. This is a show with lots of humour and rude jokes. Or you could see an opera. Opera is a Renaissance invention. It is like a play where people sing instead of talk.

But it would be a shame to miss the work of the greatest **playwright** ever. He is the English writer William Shakespeare. So switch your time machine to the city of London in England.

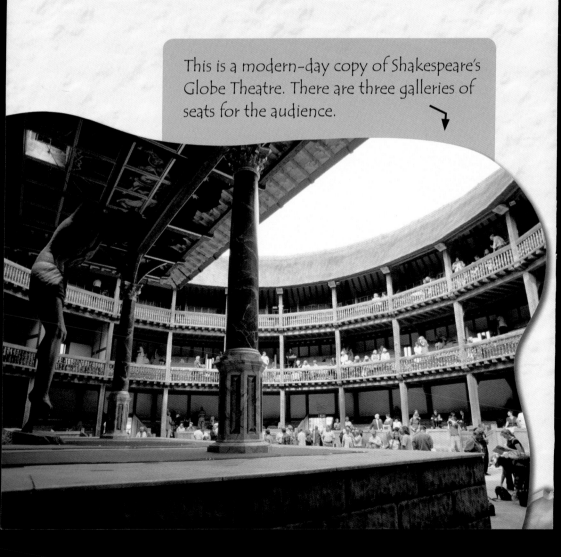

This is a modern-day copy of Shakespeare's Globe Theatre. There are three galleries of seats for the audience.

SHAKESPEARE

William Shakespeare (1564–1616) was born in
Stratford-upon-Avon. This is a country town in England.
Shakespeare moved to London to work in the theatre.
He was an actor, a theatre manager, and a playwright.
Shakespeare wrote more than 30 plays.

WILLIAM SHAKESPEARE'S GLOBE

Go back to 1600. This is more than 400 years ago.
Shakespeare is working in London. You can see his
plays performed at the city's Globe Theatre. The Globe
is a tall, round building. It has three floors of seats or
galleries. They curve around a large stage.

SEEING A PLAY

Plays at the Globe are shown in the afternoon. It costs
one penny to watch the play standing up. Wealthy
Londoners pay more to sit in the galleries. The
galleries give them protection from the rain.

Going to the theatre is a noisy and messy experience.
Everyone chats and shouts. They buy snacks to eat.
Sometimes they throw the food at the actors. People
do this if they don't like the way the actors perform.

MUSIC

Music and dancing to music are huge parts of Renaissance life. Choirs still sing in church. People also play music on the streets and at all kinds of celebrations. Renaissance Italy produces many great composers (people who write music).

This painting shows a variety of Renaissance instruments. Many of them look like modern instruments.

MUSIC FOR FUN

To hear some popular music, just stroll around Florence. Street musicians play instruments to earn a few coins. Friends entertain each other with songs. Any public show has music and dancing.

NEW MUSICAL INVENTIONS

Renaissance composers are developing new styles and ideas. An example of this is the **madrigal**. A madrigal is a song composed for several different singers. They all sing different parts. The parts all weave together.

SOME GREAT RENAISSANCE COMPOSERS

These are a few of the most famous composers of the age.

- The Gabrielis — Andrea Gabrieli (1510–1586) and his nephew Giovanni Gabrieli (c. 1555–1612). They are brilliant composers from Italy.
- Giovanni Pierluigi da Palestrina (1525–1594) — Palestrina is a very popular composer. He makes the Italian city of Rome the centre of music in Europe.
- William Byrd (1543–1623) — Byrd is a English composer of church music, songs, and madrigals.
- Claudio Monteverdi (1567–1643) — Monteverdi is a great Italian composer. He is famous for writing the first operas.

Other Italian composers are creating the first operas and ballets. A ballet is an entertainment that combines dance with music. New instruments are being invented. The first modern violins appear.

These finely dressed people are dancing at a ball in the city of Venice.

SPORTS, GAMES, AND ENTERTAINMENT

Towns and cities in Renaissance Europe have celebrations throughout the year. These may be festivals or parades. They may be sporting contests. The most important festival in Italy is Carnival. It begins in the New Year and lasts for one or two months.

During Carnival, actors put on plays. People play tricks on one another. Part of Carnival is the **masquerade**. This is when you disguise yourself with a mask (see pages 26–27). Then you can join in throwing eggs at each other.

SPORTS AND RACES

Each summer, the cities of Florence and Siena hold *Palio* festivals. The *Palio* is a horse race through the city. Riders ride without saddles.

This is a parade of horses and festival-goers. They are at the *Palio* festival in Siena, Italy.

Ball games are popular. They include a team game called *pallone*. Players use heavy paddles to hit a ball. These paddles are strapped on to their arms.

GAMES

Lots of people like to relax with a boardgame. In many European countries both adults and children play chess. People play dice and card games too. Here in Renaissance Europe, it's useful to be good at games. It will help you to make friends.

This painting shows girls playing a game of chess. It was painted about 450 years ago.

This painting shows the inside of an Italian **inn**. The men are playing boardgames.

CAFÉ CULTURE

Renaissance people love to meet up for a drink or snack. They meet at cafés, food stalls, or **taverns**. Taverns are a type of drinking house.

Cities, towns, and even small villages have taverns. Taverns serve wine or beer and some hot food. People also play cards or dice there. Sometimes they dance to music or just sit chatting.

NEW CAFÉ FASHIONS

During the Renaissance, more people are exploring the world. They are doing more business with other parts of the world. This means that new foods and drinks from foreign lands are starting to appear.

Explorers have brought back tea from China. Coffee comes from Africa and Arabia. These drinks are becoming popular in many parts of Europe. Tea and coffee are expensive though. They are both served in cafés called "coffee houses".

A TASTE OF CHOCOLATE

Chocolate is made from cocoa beans. It was first used as a drink in Central America. Spanish explorers have brought chocolate to Spain. But during the Renaissance, it is available only as a drink. Chocolate bars have not been invented yet.

DARK SECRET

Chocolate is first brought to Spain in the early 16th century. That is about 500 years ago. At first the Spanish keep it a secret. It is almost 100 years before chocolate becomes available in other parts of Europe.

SHOPPING

All types of goods from abroad (overseas countries) come into Europe through Italy. There's everything from precious stones to perfumes. So this is definitely the best place to go shopping.

These are two Renaissance pendants. They are worn on fine chains around the neck.

SHOPS, STALLS, AND MARKETS

In many Italian cities, there are often covered passageways along each side of the street. These are called **arcades**. They allow shopkeepers to display their goods in all weathers. Street stalls sell tasty snacks, such as cakes.

Cities and towns also have market days. People bring their goods to sell in the market square. You'll find wooden and leather goods. You'll find fruit and vegetables. There may even be live animals for sale.

CURRENCY AND COINS

Italian Renaissance money can be hard to understand. Each city has its own coins. Also, they keep changing in value. These are some of the coins you might use in Florence.

- *Florin*: This is a valuable gold coin.
- *Lira*: This is a silver coin. There can be between 1 and 4 *lire* in a *florin*.
- *Soldo*: There are 20 *soldi* in a *lira*.
- *Denaro*: There are 12 *denari* in a *soldo*.
- *Quattrino*: This is a coin worth 4 *denari*.

VISIT VENICE

Every May the city of Venice holds the Sensa Fair. This is an amazing shopping festival. People show the goods they've shipped from foreign lands.

These two beautiful glass goblets were made more than 530 years ago. They were made on the island of Murano, near the city of Venice. ↘

The Sensa goes on for 15 days. It attracts shoppers from all over Europe. There are also plenty of products made in Venice. The city is famous for its beautiful coloured glass.

This painting shows people travelling about the city of Venice. They are in long, flat-bottomed boats called gondolas.

CHAPTER 4

ON THE MOVE

In the Renaissance, travel isn't just about getting to the shops or visiting relatives. Explorers are setting out to sail across the world. Some aren't even sure if the Earth is round. They think they might fall off the edge if they sail too far.

Many people are travelling around Europe too. They include traders (people buying and selling goods). There are also people travelling to study or work in the great cities. Others are just sightseers. If you'd like to join them, this guide tells you how to get around. It also tells you where you can stay the night.

This picture shows a Renaissance hunting party. A wealthy lady rides in a carriage. Some of the huntsmen go on foot.

TRAVEL AND TRANSPORT

In Renaissance Italy, walking is the main way to get about. If you're on a long journey overland, you'll probably go on foot. But you might take a mule to carry your bags. For shorter journeys people sometimes use horses and carriages. For going abroad there are sailing ships.

HORSEPOWER

Horses and sometimes mules are used for riding. They are also used for pulling wagons and carriages. But this is mainly in the cities. Country roads are too muddy and full of holes. This means that carriages easily get stuck and horses get worn out. Also, horses are expensive to buy and look after.

TRAVEL BY SEA

You may want to visit other parts of Europe, such as England or Spain. To go there, you'll need to travel by sea.

By the 1500s, ships are becoming faster and better. But there aren't many special passenger ships. Instead, you pay to travel on a cargo ship. This is a ship that carries goods.

FOOD ON BOARD SHIP

Food on board ship is dreadful. You'll get smelly water and hardtack. Hardtack is a type of rock-hard biscuit. You might also get some dried peas.

Ship food is usually crawling with weevils. These are a type of beetle. Wealthy travellers prefer to take their own supply of food for the journey.

PLACES TO STAY

Journeys on foot or horseback can be very slow. They may take days or even months. So you'll need somewhere to sleep along the way.

This man is dancing to entertain the other guests at an inn.

INNS AND TAVERNS

You could stay at an **inn** or a **tavern**. An inn has lots of bedrooms. Some also have stables for horses and mules. Taverns are drinking places. But many of them also have rooms for travellers.

Some big cities have a special area full of inns and taverns. This makes it easy for newcomers to find somewhere to stay. Outside the towns, inns are usually along the main roads.

STAY AT A MONASTERY

You may be able to stay the night at a monastery. A monastery is a place where monks live and work. They often have places for visitors to sleep.

In the Renaissance, it's normal for several people to share the same bedroom. They may even share the same bed. So you'll need to careful of your belongings. You could be sharing with a criminal.

If you can't find an inn or tavern, just go to the nearest house. Ask for shelter. Many households will put up a traveller in their shed or stable.

PILGRIMAGES

A **pilgrimage** is a journey to a holy place. People go on pilgrimages for religious reasons. One of the most important places of pilgrimage is Santiago de Compostela in Spain.

People arrive at a shrine (holy place) after a long pilgrimage. Many are praying to be cured of illnesses.

EXPLORE THE WORLD

The Renaissance is a great age of exploration. Europeans explore huge parts of the world they didn't know existed.

A ROUTE TO THE EAST

Silks and spices and other precious goods come from eastern Asia. Getting them to Europe overland takes a long time. Europeans want to bring them by sea instead. But first they must find a route. This is one of the main reasons for Renaissance exploration.

The Portuguese explorer Vasco da Gama sails around the southern tip of Africa in 1497. This is more than 500 years ago. His journey opens up a sea route to India and eastern Asia.

During the Renaissance, Europeans are making proper world maps for the first time. This map was drawn in 1536. This is more than 470 years ago.

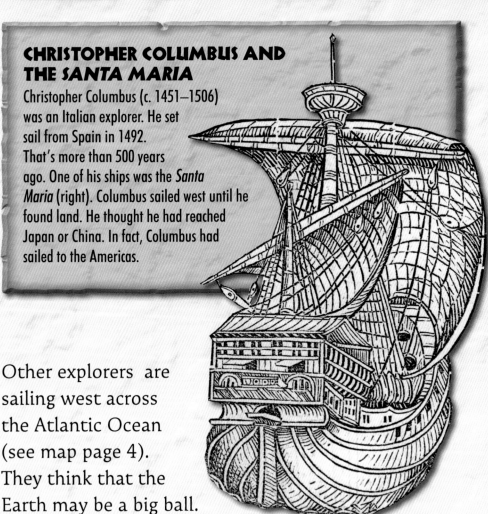

CHRISTOPHER COLUMBUS AND THE *SANTA MARIA*

Christopher Columbus (c. 1451–1506) was an Italian explorer. He set sail from Spain in 1492. That's more than 500 years ago. One of his ships was the *Santa Maria* (right). Columbus sailed west until he found land. He thought he had reached Japan or China. In fact, Columbus had sailed to the Americas.

Other explorers are sailing west across the Atlantic Ocean (see map page 4). They think that the Earth may be a big ball. They plan to reach the East by sailing around it.

AROUND THE WORLD IN 1,080 DAYS

The Portuguese explorer Ferdinand Magellan sets sail from Spain in 1519. This is almost 500 years ago. The voyage takes almost three years. It is the first ever round-the-world trip. Magellan is killed during the voyage.

This painting shows the arrest and execution of Sir Thomas More. He was a British politician and writer. Sir Thomas was punished for disagreeing with the English king Henry VIII.

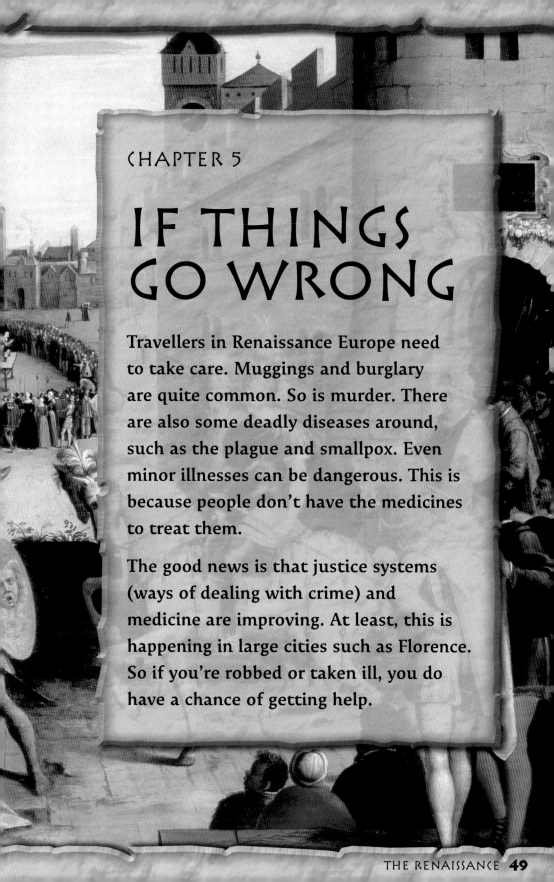

CHAPTER 5

IF THINGS GO WRONG

Travellers in Renaissance Europe need to take care. Muggings and burglary are quite common. So is murder. There are also some deadly diseases around, such as the plague and smallpox. Even minor illnesses can be dangerous. This is because people don't have the medicines to treat them.

The good news is that justice systems (ways of dealing with crime) and medicine are improving. At least, this is happening in large cities such as Florence. So if you're robbed or taken ill, you do have a chance of getting help.

CRIME AND PUNISHMENT

There's a lot of crime in Renaissance Italy. So you'll need to hold on to your bag. Also, make sure you stay out of trouble. The punishments are very unpleasant.

OUT AND ABOUT

Travellers need to be very careful. Robbers lie in wait along the roads. Some innkeepers steal from their guests. There is a lot of violence too. There are many murders.

PUNISHMENTS

- **Stocks**: This is a type of wooden frame. For small crimes, you might have your feet or arms locked in the stocks for a few hours. People can pelt you with rotten food.
- **Amputations**: Sometimes a person's hands, ears, or nose are cut off.
- **Flogging/whipping**: Being beaten with a whip or a stick is a common punishment.
- **Hanging**: This is the usual method of execution.
- **Beheading**: This is having your head chopped off.
- **Being hanged, drawn, and quartered**: A person is hanged until almost dead. Then their guts are cut out. The body is then cut into four.

ARE YOU A CRIMINAL?

You can get into big trouble if anyone thinks you are a **heretic**. A heretic is someone who disagrees with the Church. There is an organization (group) in Italy that works to find heretics. It is called the Holy Inquisition.

JUSTICE SYSTEM

In Italy, each city has its own police force. The police are often cruel and dishonest. They can arrest anyone they believe may be guilty of a crime.

The suspect (person believed to be guilty) goes to court. This is where judges listen to what the suspect and other people have to say. The judges decide on punishments.

This painting shows lawyers in their office. Lawyers are people who know all about the law (rules of the country). People pay them to help win court cases.

ILLNESSES AND MEDICINES

If you get ill in Renaissance Italy, you'll have a huge choice of treatments. You can choose which type of treatment you believe in. But this has to be a type that you can afford.

DOCTORS AND HEALERS

Sick people can pay to see a proper doctor. This is someone who has studied medicine at university. There are also hospitals where doctors look after the poor and sick.

For everyday illnesses and injuries you need a barber-surgeon. Barbers do not only cut hair. They sew up wounds and fix broken bones. They also do "bloodletting". This means cutting the patient's arm to let out blood. People believe that bloodletting can cure many illnesses.

This picture shows an apothecary at work. He is weighing out a medicine for a customer.

This book is about plants that can be used as medicines. It is open at a page that describes the uses of the herb sage.

You can get medicines from an **apothecary** or a **herbalist**. These are people who prepare medicines with herbs and other materials.

IDEAS ABOUT MEDICINE

Renaissance doctors still have some wrong ideas about what causes illness. But scientists are beginning to learn more. They are learning by studying the body closely.

RENAISSANCE REMEDIES

Here are a few treatments recommended for medical problems:

- Skin rash: Rub with dock-leaf juice mixed with vinegar.
- Scrofula (a skin disease): This is thought to be cured by the touch of a king.
- Common cold: Put chopped turnip up your nose.
- Headache: Put a tin pot on your head and pour hot liquid lead into it.

This painted panel shows St John the Divine. It was painted by Sandro Botticelli more than 500 years ago. He was one of the most famous Renaissance artists.

CHAPTER 6

USEFUL INFORMATION

This section contains some useful facts and figures. You can use it to check up on some of the most important Renaissance people. You can see at a glance what happened when during the Renaissance. There's also a section explaining how the Renaissance ended.

WHO'S WHO?

Here's a quick guide to some famous people of the Renaissance.

The Borgias: The Italian Borgia family were famous for their greed and their murdering. Cesare Borgia (1475–1507) was the son of **Pope** Alexander VI. He became leader of the Pope's armies. His sister Lucrezia was a great **patron** of artists (see page 29).

Filippo Brunelleschi (1377–1446): Brunelleschi was an Italian artist and **architect** (designer of buildings). He designed the famous egg-shaped dome of Florence's cathedral (see page 10). Brunelleschi based his style on ancient Roman buildings.

Isabella d'Este (1474–1539): Isabella came from a wealthy Italian family. She used her money to make the Italian city of Mantua a great centre of art and music. It was also a great centre of writing.

Henry the Navigator (1394–1460): Henry was a Portuguese prince. He organized and paid for explorations along the African coast.

King Henry VIII (1491–1547): Henry VIII was an English king. He was very interested in Renaissance ideas. Henry spent huge sums of money on art, music, and architecture.

The Medicis: The Medicis were Florence's richest and most powerful family. Lorenzo de' Medici (1449-1492) practically ruled Florence. He was a great patron of art and science.

Michelangelo Buonarroti (1475–1564): Michelangelo was an Italian sculptor, painter, and architect. He was thought to be the greatest artist of his time. One of his most famous works was the painted ceiling and wall of the Sistine Chapel. This was the pope's chapel in the city of Rome.

SOME RENAISSANCE FESTIVALS

These are some festivals celebrated in Renaissance times. Some took place only in Italy. Others took place all over Europe.

Date	Name	What happens?
6 January	Epiphany	Processions (parades), music, and feasting
New Year—Lent	Carnival	Parties and dancing. Dressing up and playing tricks. This takes place in Italy.
March or April	Holy Week	Religious processions and plays
March or April	Easter	Church services and feasting
1 May	May Day	Dancing in the streets
May	Sensa Fair	Shopping festival in Venice, Italy
24 June	St John's Day	*Palio* horse race in Florence, Italy

WHAT HAPPENED TO THE RENAISSANCE?

The Renaissance didn't have a definite start or end point. It reached its height at different times in different places.

PROBLEMS FOR ITALY

In Italy, the Renaissance was at its height in the late 1400s and early 1500s. That's about 500 years ago. This was a time of great achievements in science and the arts. But at the same time, events were bringing the Renaissance to an end.

An Italian named Savonarola spoke out against Renaissance fashions and art. He said they were ungodly. At about the same time, other European countries began attacking Italy.

Artists, writers, and scientists were still working in Italy. But war made life much harder for them.

EUROPE AND THE WORLD

European explorers found new sea routes. Goods no longer had to travel to Europe through Italy. Now ships could carry them to cities such as Lisbon in Portugal and London in England. Italy became less important to the rest of Europe.

Some Italian artists and scientists moved to other European countries. They continued their work there.

In 1527 German armies destroyed much of the city of Rome. After this, several Italian artists were invited to France. They were asked to decorate a great country house called the Chateau of Fontainebleau. From there, Italian Renaissance ideas spread through Europe.

THE ENLIGHTENMENT

The Renaissance in Europe ended in the 1650s. That's about 350 years ago. It slowly changed into another period. The new period is known as the Enlightenment.

The Renaissance had been a time of great progress in science. But it was also a time when people still believed in witches and magic. Religious belief often clashed with the work of scientists.

During the Enlightenment, science became more important. The artistic side of the Renaissance became less important. The Enlightenment carried the world towards modern times.

THE RENAISSANCE AT A GLANCE

TIMELINE

AD 1304	Writer Francesco Petrarch, "father of the Renaissance", is born near Florence in Italy.
Around 1420	Henry the Navigator pays for voyages of exploration to explore the coast of Africa.
1434–1464	Cosimo de' Medici controls Florence.
1452	Leonardo da Vinci, artist, scientist, and inventor, is born near Florence.
1450s	First printing of the Gutenberg Bible on Gutenberg's printing press.
1469–1492	Lorenzo de' Medici controls Florence. He becomes a **patron** (supporter) of the arts.
1475	Artist Michelangelo Buonarroti is born near Florence.
1492	Christopher Columbus sails to the Americas.
1494	France invades Italy. The Medici family loses power.
1494–1498	Girolamo Savonarola controls Florence.
1497	Vasco da Gama sails around southern Africa.
1501–1504	Michelangelo carves his sculpture *David*.
1503–1506	Leonardo da Vinci paints the *Mona Lisa*.
1509–1547	Reign of King Henry VIII in England.
1517	Martin Luther challenges the Catholic Church.
1519	Ferdinand Magellan sets sail on the first round-the-world journey.
1527	German and Spanish armies move into Rome.
1543	Copernicus publishes his theory that the Earth moves around the Sun.
1564	Galileo Galilei, scientist and inventor, is born in Italy.
1564	William Shakespeare, **playwright**, is born in England.
1608	Hans Lippershey invents the telescope.
1629–1631	The plague (a killer disease) breaks out in Italy.
1633	Galileo is on trial in Rome for supporting Copernicus.

FURTHER READING

BOOKS

Copernicus: founder of Modern Astronomy (Great Minds of Science) Catherine M. Andronik (Enslow Publishers, 2006)

Eyewitness: Renaissance, Alison Cole (Dorling Kindersley, 2000)

Leonardo Da Vinci, Andrew Langley (Dorling Kindersley, 2006)

Michelangelo (Signature Lives Renaissance Era), Barbara A. Somervill (Compass Point Books, 2005)

WEBSITES

- www.twingroves.district96.k12.il.us/Renaissance/
  GeneralFiles/RenLinksGen.html
  This website has links to sites all about everyday life in the Renaissance.

- www.learner.org/exhibits/renaissance/florence.html
  This site offers information on daily life, politics, and art in Renaissance Florence.

- www.mos.org/sln/Leonardo/
  This is a multimedia site on Leonardo da Vinci.

Disclaimer

All the Internet addresses (URLs) given in this book were valid at the time of going to press. However, due to the dynamic nature of the Internet, some addresses may have changed, or sites may have changed or ceased to exist since publication. While the author and publishers regret any inconvenience this may cause readers, no responsibility for any such changes can be accepted by either the author or the publishers.

GLOSSARY

apothecary old word for someone who mixes and sells medicines

arcade covered passage, especially one with shops or stalls on one or both sides

architect someone who designs buildings

city-state territory or land with its own government and laws. It is made up of a city together with the smaller towns and countryside that surround it.

commedia dell'arte Italian form of theatre similar to pantomime. It involves cartoonish characters, silly jokes, and comedy violence.

doublet type of close-fitting waistcoat or jacket

galleries raised areas of seating. They are built onto the inside wall of a theatre.

herbalist someone who makes medicines using plants

heretic someone who disagrees with or argues against a set of beliefs, especially religious teachings

humanism system of thought that values human feelings and ideas. It places less importance on religious ideas or obedience to leaders.

inn place where travellers pay to stay for the night. Some inns have stables for horses and mules.

madrigal song with several parts that weave together

masquerade celebration in which people wear masks as a disguise

patron someone who pays an artist or scientist to work for them

patronage when someone pays for and supports an artist or scientist

pilgrimage journey to a holy place or shrine

playwright someone who writes plays

pope leader of the Catholic Church

Protestantism branch of Christianity that developed during the Renaissance

republic state or country that has no king or queen. It elects, or chooses, its leaders

stocks type of locking clamp used to imprison people

tavern place where people go to drink, chat, and play games. Many taverns also have bedrooms where travellers can stay the night.

INDEX